CW01512601

Original title:
Echoes of the Soul's Flame

Author: Olivia Orav
ISBN HARDBACK: 978-1-80561-194-3
ISBN PAPERBACK: 978-1-80561-755-6

Golden Standards of Affection

In gardens lush, our laughter grows,
Tender whispers, where the sunlight glows.
Fingers intertwined, a sacred bond,
In every heartbeat, love grows fond.

Days melt like gold in evening light,
Promises gleam, guiding through the night.
With every glance, a story told,
Warmth of affection, more precious than gold.

Lingering Warmth of the Past

In faded photographs, our smiles remain,
Echoes of laughter dance through the rain.
Time slips away, yet memories bind,
In the heart's quiet corners, love we find.

Whispers of old songs in the evening air,
Carried by breezes, sweet and rare.
Each stolen moment, a gentle embrace,
Lingering warmth we cannot replace.

The Reflection of Bold Flames

Fires blaze with a fierce delight,
Casting shadows that dance in the night.
Heat of passion, burning bright,
Guiding lost souls towards the light.

In embers' glow, dreams take flight,
Illuminated paths weave futures right.
Through trials faced, emboldened we stand,
Reflecting strength, hand in hand.

Shining Within the Shadows

In secret corners where silence dwells,
Soft whispers echo, casting their spells.
Amid the gloom, a light breaks free,
Hope shines bright for all to see.

Hidden messages dance on the breeze,
Encouraging hearts, putting minds at ease.
In shadows deep, love knows its way,
Guiding lost spirits to brighter days.

Heart's Ambers in the Night

In shadows cast by moonlight bright,
The whispers of a love take flight.
From ashes soft, a glow remains,
Embers dance through heart's refrains.

The gentle breeze, it calls your name,
Filling the dark with warmth and flame.
Each flicker tells a silent tale,
Of passions lost that never pale.

Beneath the stars, our secrets weave,
In every spark, we dare believe.
Through time's embrace, we find our way,
In heart's ambers, forever stay.

Hues of a Hidden Flame

Deep within where shadows blend,
A hidden flame, my heart's true friend.
With colors rich, it softly glows,
In every hue, a story flows.

Cerulean dreams and crimson sighs,
In this place, our spirits rise.
Each shade is brush upon the night,
Painting paths of love's delight.

When daylight fades, the fire ignites,
Casting warmth on quiet nights.
In whispered hues, we find our peace,
Our souls in flames shall never cease.

Fables of the Living Fire

In flickering tales, our fables bloom,
From kindled sparks, we chase the gloom.
Each tale a thread of life's design,
Woven through dusk, adorned in pine.

The fire tells of joy and plight,
Of dances held in the soft twilight.
With every pop, a wish ignites,
In living fire, our spirits light.

Through ancient woods and whispered dreams,
In every ember, the world redeems.
Together we write our boundless lore,
In fables of fire, forevermore.

Illuminated Echoes

In quiet corners, echoes dwell,
Illuminated by stories we tell.
From shadows deep, they ripple wide,
A chorus of hearts where dreams reside.

These golden lights in the stillness hum,
A melody of where we come from.
Through time's embrace, the echoes ring,
In every note, our souls take wing.

Moments captured in softest glow,
Illuminated paths where we go.
With every echo, a memory's flight,
Guiding us gently through the night.

Radiance of the Inner Self

In silence blooms the light within,
A quiet spark, a gentle grin,
Reflecting dreams of hope untold,
A warmth that never grows too cold.

Each thought a beam, each wish a hue,
Colors of life, both bright and true,
A dance of shadows, a leap of grace,
Embracing all in the heart's space.

The whispers echo through the night,
With courage gathered, take to flight,
A journey deep, where secrets dwell,
The radiance of the inner self.

From depths of soul, a treasure gleams,
A world awash with vibrant dreams,
Awake the spirit, let it soar,
Unveil the light forever more.

In every heartbeat, truth will sing,
An infinite joy that love can bring,
Connected threads, a tapestry,
The radiant self, wild and free.

A Symphony of Glows

Beneath the stars, a symphony plays,
In rhythms soft, it gently sways,
Glows of warmth in the night's embrace,
A magic touch, a sacred space.

Each note a whisper, sweet and light,
Resonates deep through the quiet night,
A melody of hearts entwined,
In perfect harmony, unconfined.

With every breath, a story told,
In chords that shimmer, bright and bold,
Through valleys low and mountains high,
The symphony of glows will fly.

The dawn awakens, a brand new song,
Guiding souls, where dreams belong,
In unity, we rise and lift,
A gift of love, our greatest gift.

Together we dance in the sun's warm glow,
Creating music that only we know,
In symphonies bright, we find our way,
Illuminated hearts shall never sway.

The Fire Within

A flicker starts, a hidden spark,
A silent flame ignites the dark,
With every breath, it swells and grows,
A radiant heart, the fire shows.

Embers dance in the quiet night,
Illuminating paths with inner light,
The warmth of passion, fierce and free,
Encased in dreams, it longs to be.

Through trials faced, the blaze endures,
With strength found deep in hidden cures,
It fuels the spirit, breaks the chains,
In every joy, in every pain.

So stoke the flame, let it inspire,
Transform your soul, ignite your fire,
For from the ashes, life begins,
In every heart, the fire wins.

Let it guide you on the road ahead,
Through darkness vast and whispers said,
For in the heart, the fire's glow,
Is all you need, to rise and flow.

Threads of a Burning Narrative

In every tale, the threads intertwine,
A tapestry woven with love divine,
Each moment captured, a vivid scene,
A burning narrative, rich and keen.

Through pages turned, the whispers sing,
Of fleeting dreams, and the hope they bring,
The fabric holds the stories dear,
In every stitch, the heart draws near.

With colors bold, and shades of gray,
Each thread a choice that lights the way,
In the loom of time, we craft our fate,
A dance of shadows that we create.

From dusk till dawn, the stories flow,
In every heartbeat, life will glow,
A quilt of memories, soft and warm,
The burning narrative, a living form.

So weave your tale with passion bright,
Embrace the joy, the sorrow, the fight,
For in the threads, the truth shall dwell,
A burning narrative, weaved so well.

The Spark That Never Fades

In the depths of night, a glow,
A flicker dances, soft and slow.
It whispers tales of dreams long gone,
A beacon bright, a love still drawn.

Through storms that rage and shadows cast,
The spark remains, a flame steadfast.
It warms the heart, it lights the way,
A guiding force, come what may.

Forever burned, through time and space,
In memory's vault, it finds its place.
Though winds may chill and times may change,
This spark endures, it won't estrange.

In every laugh, in every tear,
It flickers close, forever near.
A promise held, by fate embraced,
In silent nights, the spark's interlaced.

So when the world feels cold and dim,
Recall that flame, keep hope within.
The spark that lives, it never fades,
In every heart, its light parades.

Chasing the Glowing Remember There

In twilight's grasp, we search the skies,
For glowing echoes, love's replies.
They shimmer softly, gently sway,
Reminders of a brighter day.

With every heartbeat, whispers call,
To chase the light, to never fall.
A journey forged through darkened lands,
With hope as guide and fate in hands.

Remember there, where dreams are spun,
In the warmth of a setting sun.
Each star a promise, glints of gold,
A tapestry of stories told.

We wander trails both old and new,
With every step, the glow breaks through.
Chasing shadows, longing's fire,
Bound to the glow, we never tire.

So find the light in any place,
Embrace the warmth, the sweet embrace.
Chasing memories, shining bright,
A path illuminated, pure delight.

The Glow of Silent Longing

In quiet corners, shadows sigh,
A gentle ache, a lonesome cry.
The glow of hope, both faint and clear,
It beckons softly, drawing near.

In dreams we wander, hearts align,
With whispered wishes, hands entwine.
Though silence reigns, our spirits soar,
In longing's grip, we crave for more.

A tender light, through dark it weaves,
In every heart, a love believes.
The glow persists, through night and day,
In silent spaces, it finds its way.

We hold the moments, cherish deep,
In longing's arms, our secrets keep.
Across the distance, hearts ignite,
The glow that thrives in endless night.

So let it shine, this glow of ours,
In garden dreams, amongst the stars.
Through silent longing, we will find,
A love eternal, heart aligned.

Breaths of Eternal Heat

In the warmth of dawn, a fire ignites,
Breaths of life, in golden lights.
Through echoes past, the heat remains,
A rhythm flowed in love's refrains.

Underneath the vast expanse,
In every glance, a tireless dance.
The warmth flows deep, igniting dreams,
In whispered words, in sunlight beams.

With every heartbeat, embers glow,
Through trials faced, the warmth will grow.
Together bound, through thick and thin,
In breaths of heat, we find our kin.

As seasons shift and shadows play,
The fire within won't drift away.
In every moment, our hearts pulse true,
Eternal heat, a bond renewed.

So breathe it in, this warmth divine,
Through every storm, our spirits shine.
In love's embrace, life's sweetest feat,
We live forever in this heat.

The Unseen Fire Within

In shadows deep, where whispers dwell,
The heart ignites, a silent spell.
A flicker glows, unseen, yet bright,
A flame that dances, soft with light.

Bound by the chains of doubt and fear,
The fire breathes, it draws us near.
It warms the cold, ignites the soul,
A guiding force that makes us whole.

In stillness found, a gentle heat,
Within resides, no need for feat.
Through storms and trials, it will spark,
A beacon shining in the dark.

From ashes rise, the spirit fierce,
The fire's touch, our wounds it pierce.
In every heart, its glow will sway,
A hidden truth that lights the way.

So let it burn, this unseen fire,
With every breath, we climb higher.
Embrace its warmth, let doubts confine,
We are the flames that intertwine.

In Quest of Shimmering Truths

Beneath the stars, we seek the light,
In shadows cast, we chase the night.
Each twinkling gem, a riddle deep,
In silence held, the cosmos speaks.

With every step, the path unfolds,
A tapestry of tales retold.
The questions asked, the whispers soft,
In questing hearts, the truth aloft.

Through mountains high and valleys low,
The shimmering truths begin to glow.
In every soul, a spark we find,
A mirror held to all mankind.

So let us wander, hand in hand,
Through tangled woods, across the land.
With eyes wide open, hearts sincere,
The shimmering truths will draw us near.

And in the end, we'll understand,
The journey's worth was not so planned.
Each truth we find, a jewel bright,
In quest of shimmering, radiant light.

An Ember's Silent Prayer

In twilight's hush, a whisper soft,
An ember glows, aloft, aloft.
With every breath, it sways with grace,
A quiet plea in this vast space.

The darkness folds, the shadows creep,
Yet through the night, its secrets seep.
A silent prayer on the breeze,
In flickers caught, the heart's unease.

As flicker fades, the warmth remains,
In solitude, the ember gains.
A hope ignites from deep within,
A tender light where dreams begin.

With every spark, the spirit thrives,
In silent prayers, the soul derives.
From embered glow to radiant flare,
We find our strength in silent prayer.

A call to arms, a gentle fight,
To guard the flame, to share the light.
For every heart that dares to dream,
An ember's prayer can softly beam.

The Forge of Inner Light

In the depths of night, the forge awaits,
Where dreams are shaped, and fate creates.
With hammer's strike and fire's glow,
We mold our paths, and courage grows.

Through molten tears, the metal bends,
With every beat, a journey mends.
From forge to fate, the steel ignites,
Our inner light in darkest nights.

As sparks take flight, we find our way,
In trials faced, we grow, we sway.
With fiery heart, we brave the storm,
In the forge of light, we find our form.

Each scar will tell a tale, profound,
Of battles fought, where strength is found.
In every crack, a chance to grow,
The forge within forever glows.

So wield the hammer, shape the fate,
In the forge of light, it's never late.
With every strike, our spirits rise,
Creating worlds beneath the skies.

Dance of the Forgotten Sparks

In twilight's glow, they start to rise,
Whispers of dreams that fill the skies.
Old memories twirl in the evening's grace,
Silent echoes in a long-lost place.

Each flicker tells of love and pain,
A dance of joy, and yet of stain.
Beneath the stars, they twist and twine,
Forgotten sparks in liquid time.

They shimmer bright, yet fade away,
In shadows cast by the light of day.
Each moment caught, a fleeting art,
The dance of dreams within the heart.

So let them dance, this silent crew,
In every heart, they find a view.
Of hopes reborn, of wishes cast,
A fleeting spark that cannot last.

In twilight's glow, they weave and sway,
A timeless tale that will not fray.
In memories held, they leap and spin,
The dance of sparks that lie within.

Resonance of the Heart's Fire

In quiet beats, a rhythm sings,
A melody of fragile strings.
Each pulse reflects the love's embrace,
Within the depths, in sacred space.

The flames arise with gentle might,
Igniting dreams in the velvet night.
A warmth that glows, a fire bright,
Enfolding souls in soft delight.

Resonant whispers flow and glide,
With every spark, we come alive.
Unfolding passion, deep and vast,
The heart's fire burn, forever cast.

So let the warmth ignite our song,
In every echo, we belong.
In harmony, we'll rise and soar,
The heart's fire, we can't ignore.

With each heartbeat, love's essence flows,
A dance of embers, gently glows.
In every breath, we find our way,
A resonance that's here to stay.

Flickers of Timeless Passion

In shadowed corners, secrets play,
Flickers of light in bright array.
Whispers of hearts entwined in fate,
A timeless passion, never too late.

Each spark ignites the dormant soul,
Illuminating what makes us whole.
In tender moments, the dance begins,
A journey shared through losses and wins.

With eyes that speak the silent truth,
In fleeting glances, recapture youth.
The fire within, forever remains,
In every joy, in every pains.

As time flows on, the embers glow,
In every flicker, love's glow we show.
A tale as old as time can weave,
In passion's grip, we still believe.

So let the flickers lead us near,
To realms of love, to roots sincere.
In whispered breath and soft caress,
Timeless passion, forever bless.

Flames Beneath the Surface

Beneath the waves, the heat resides,
A tumultuous dance where wonder hides.
Unseen embers pulse with life's embrace,
Subtle flames in a secret space.

Each flicker stirs the depths of night,
Awakens whispers, a silent fight.
Compelling tides that churn and sway,
Flooded with dreams that cannot stray.

In shadows' realm, the fire is bold,
Stories of heat and color told.
A brilliance stirs, fierce and untamed,
As midnight's glow cannot be named.

From deep below, the flames will rise,
Erupting forth beneath the skies.
In every spark, a world unfolds,
The dance of flames, a tale retold.

So let us glimpse what lies beneath,
In fiery depths where passions breathe.
For every flame, a heart ignites,
Beneath the surface, love ignites.

Flickering Memories

In the corners of my mind, they play,
Soft whispers of a distant day.
Laughter dances on the breeze,
Echoes wrapped in time's gentle freeze.

Faded images, bright and clear,
Holding close what I hold dear.
Each touch of light, a fleeting glance,
A haunting song, a timeless dance.

The warmth of sun on skin once felt,
In the silence, where secrets dwelt.
A tapestry of stories spun,
In the twilight, when day is done.

Yet some may fade, like stars at dawn,
But in my heart, they're never gone.
With every flicker, they call my name,
In the shadows, they still flame.

Hold them close, lest they be lost,
In the echoes, I count the cost.
These memories, a sacred thread,
Binding all that I have shed.

Glances of a Burning Spirit

Through the flicker of candlelight,
A spirit dances, bold and bright.
With every glance, the world ignites,
In dreams woven through long nights.

Eyes that shine with untamed fire,
Whispers of passion, deep desire.
Each flicker tells a tale untold,
Of hearts that dare, of souls that bold.

A flicker here, a spark to chase,
In the shadows, we find our place.
In glances shared, a promise made,
As histories of heartbeats fade.

The spirit burns with fierce intent,
A guiding light, a firm ascent.
With every glance, the flames will grow,
In the dance of life, we ebb and flow.

Ember eyes that pierce the night,
With every glance, we take to flight.
Awakened hearts, a cosmic pull,
In the fire, we are made whole.

Flames of Unseen Desires

Beneath the surface, passions reign,
Where silence masks an aching pain.
Flames flicker in the darkened heart,
Unseen desires, a work of art.

In quiet moments, secrets swell,
Like whispered dreams that yearn to tell.
In shadowed corners, hope will rise,
In every breath, the spark defies.

A glance, a touch, a fleeting sigh,
In hidden depths, we learn to fly.
The heart's true fire, potent and pure,
In the silent night, we find our cure.

With every pulse, the yearning grows,
In the chaos, the secret glows.
Chasing shadows, embracing light,
These unseen flames guide us through night.

In every laugh, in every tear,
The flames of desire draw us near.
With hearts ablaze, we'll find our way,
In the warmth of love that will not sway.

The Warmth of Unspoken Dreams

In the quiet, dreams take flight,
Wrapped in shadows, kissed by light.
Unspoken wishes, soft and sweet,
A warmth that makes us feel complete.

With every sigh, a hope is born,
In the silence, a heart is worn.
Through uncharted paths we roam,
In the warmth, we craft our home.

Each whispered thought, a tender thread,
Linger long, where angels tread.
Unfelt feelings weave the night,
In the distance, a flickering light.

Close your eyes, let the silence breathe,
In these dreams, we find reprieve.
The warmth of love, yet to be shared,
In the soul, we have declared.

With gentle grace, our spirits soar,
Amongst the stars, forevermore.
In unspoken dreams, hand in hand,
We carve our fate, we take our stand.

Illumination Beneath the Skin

Soft whispers pulse, a glow ignites,
In shadows deep, where secrets dwell.
Each heartbeat sings, revealing sights,
The tender light, a silent bell.

Flickering dreams, beneath our seams,
In every scar, a tale unfolds.
With every breath, a spark redeems,
The warmth of truth, the warmth of souls.

Faint glimmers dance, on paths unseen,
Through valleys dark, and endless night.
In whispered breaths, the spaces between,
Beneath the skin, the world feels right.

Every heartbeat, a histories thread,
Interwoven tales of love and pain.
In the quiet, hear the words unsaid,
Illumination from joy and strain.

In depths we find, the light we seek,
A fire kindled, both fierce and fair.
The brilliance shines, when voices speak,
Illumination, forever there.

A Journey with Sparks

Embers dance in the midnight air,
With laughter bright, we chase the stars.
A journey vast, without a care,
Together weaving, time is ours.

Each step we take ignites a flame,
Moments shared, like drops of rain.
In every glance, a whispered name,
A tapestry of joy and pain.

Through winding trails, the sparks will guide,
Unseen paths filled with light and grace.
In every stride, we turn the tide,
Together in this endless space.

With flickers bright, our hearts align,
As dreams unfold in the darkened skies.
Through every trial, our stars will shine,
In this embrace, our spirits rise.

And in the distance, stars will chart,
The journey forged by sparks and breath.
In every heartbeat, a brand new start,
A blazing tale that conquers death.

The Heat of Untold Stories

Underneath the weight of night,
There's warmth that breathes, that lingers long.
With every glance, a hidden light,
The heat of tales, unsung, yet strong.

Echoes whisper through the years,
Loud yet soft, like morning dew.
In every laugh, a trace of tears,
The heat ignites what feels so true.

In twilight's hush, we share our sighs,
With open hearts, we brave the dark.
Each story holds the ancient wise,
The heat of life, a constant spark.

Through winding roads, and shadows cast,
We weave together, the threads of fate.
Each moment carved, forever last,
The heat within, we cannot wait.

In the silence where dreams reside,
Untold stories start to breathe.
With every pulse, our souls collide,
The heat of life, we can't believe.

Traces of Ashes and Light

In the afterglow of what has been,
The memories linger, soft yet bright.
With traces found where hopes have been,
In shadows dense, we seek the light.

Ashes scattered across the past,
Tell stories of what once was free.
In every flicker, shadows cast,
A dance of dark and light to see.

The warmth of fire, the chill of night,
In contrast varies our gentle touch.
With every warmth, a chance for flight,
Traces linger, they mean so much.

Beneath the stars, the world awakes,
With whispers soft, the past ignites.
In every heart, the journey makes,
A blend of ashes and glowing lights.

To find the beauty in what remains,
The echoes of both loss and love.
In every soul, the silent gains,
Traces of ashes, light from above.

Illuminations of the Inner Horizon

In shadows deep, a flicker shows,
A path unfolds where stillness grows.
Beyond the veil, the vision clear,
Awakens dreams we hold so dear.

With every breath, the light expands,
Embracing whispers in our hands.
A dance of sparks, the heart ignites,
Illuminating endless sights.

The silent echoes softly call,
Reminding us we rise, we fall.
But in the depths, a flame persists,
Guiding souls through morning mists.

In twilight's grace, the secrets play,
As colors weave the night and day.
With every step, we're drawn within,
To find the truths that breathe, begin.

The inner horizon lights the day,
With every glance, it will convey.
A journey bright, through shadows cast,
We find our way, we journey fast.

Murmurs Between the Ashes

In quiet places where shadows dwell,
The whispered tales begin to swell.
Amongst the ruins, life will sigh,
Murmurs of love refuse to die.

The embers glow with stories spun,
Of battles fought, of races run.
In fragile hearts, the hope will rise,
Like phoenix wings against the skies.

Each flicker tells of loss and grace,
Rekindling dreams we dare embrace.
So gather near, to share the fire,
And listen close, to hearts' desire.

The silence speaks in whispered tones,
Of broken hearts and aching bones.
But in the ashes, life finds way,
To bloom anew in bright array.

With every breath, we find the strength,
To rise again, to go the length.
For murmurings of days gone by,
Will light the night and lift the sky.

Songs of the Soul's Radiance

In twilight's hush, a melody,
Resonates with harmony.
Notes of love weave through the air,
Each longing heart finds solace there.

Voices rise like silver streams,
In whispered vows and cherished dreams.
The soul's radiance shines so bright,
Guiding hearts through darkest night.

With every chord, we break the mold,
In stories of the brave and bold.
Each song a bridge, a leap of trust,
Uniting souls with love, a must.

In every rhythm, heartbeats sway,
A dance of light, come what may.
With every note, the spirit sings,
Of endless hope that truly wings.

For in the music, we find grace,
A mirror to our warm embrace.
The songs of souls will ever bloom,
A fragrant love that knows no gloom.

Glimmers of Lost Wishes

A flicker dims in quiet space,
Where dreams once danced in boundless grace.
Glimmers of hopes long turned to dust,
Yet deep within, we still we trust.

In moonlit nights, the stars remind,
Of wishes whispered, left behind.
Yet in the dark, new paths arise,
As shadows share their soft replies.

With every tear, a seed is sown,
In fertile ground where love is grown.
Though wishes fade, new dreams will glow,
As life unfolds, we learn to flow.

In laughter's wake, the past will blend,
With memories that seem to bend.
Glimmers of lost wishes remain,
Transforming hurt to joy through pain.

So gather near, let's share the light,
Embrace the journey, take the flight.
In every glimmer, there's a tale,
Of wishes lost that still prevail.

The Serenade of Fading Lights

In twilight's gentle embrace, we rest,
Soft whispers coat the velvet sky.
Stars play the notes of a distant quest,
As shadows breathe their silent sigh.

Memories dance on the edge of night,
Each flicker tells a story untold.
In the glow, hearts take flight,
While time weaves dreams in threads of gold.

The moonlight spills like a silver frost,
Wrapping the earth in tender grace.
In this moment, nothing is lost,
For the stars are here to embrace.

With every note, a promise glows,
In echoes of a love once bright.
Beneath the serenade, our spirit flows,
As we hold tight to fading light.

Chronicles of Silent Heat

In shadows deep, the embers whisper,
A tale of passion, unspoken, wild.
Heat radiates, no touch is crisper,
In silence, two hearts remain beguiled.

The night breathes warmth, an unchained fire,
Where glances spark like thunder's roar.
In every sigh, we climb higher,
Seeking solace on this secret floor.

A flicker in time, a transient glow,
Tangled in dreams, we grasp the heat.
The world fades back, a forgotten show,
As we dance to rhythms bittersweet.

The chronicles go, but words cannot tell,
Of the fervor wrapped in sacred air.
In this silence, we live so well,
Resistant to the burdens we bear.

Beneath the Veil of Flickering Hues

Under a sky of shifting shades,
We wander where colors softly blend.
Every shadow, a mystery fades,
In the twilight, our thoughts transcend.

Brush strokes of dusk sweep the land,
Orange to blue, a painter's dream.
With each hue, we weave our strand,
Bound by the softest twilight seam.

Caught in a waltz of light's embrace,
We share whispers, tender and light.
In this palette, time finds its place,
As stars awake to welcome the night.

Through flickering hues, our souls ignite,
In a tapestry spun from the glow.
Beneath the veil, we lose all fright,
Together, free, with nowhere to go.

Whispers of a Smoldering Heart

In the quiet, embers softly hum,
A heart once fierce, now whispers low.
Memories linger, like a beating drum,
In the silence, love continues to grow.

Smoke rises in curls, delicate grace,
Each exhale carries a story deep.
Lost in reverie, we find our place,
In the warmth, a promise we keep.

Through the haze, a flicker of fate,
Guides us gently to where dreams collide.
In every pulse, we navigate,
Painting our secrets with fervent pride.

The smoldering heart knows no retreat,
For in the whispers lies our truth.
With every beat, the rhythm's sweet,
In passion's fire, we find our youth.

The Play of Light and Shadow

In the dance of dusk, shadows sway,
Figures fade and colors play,
Whispers of twilight weave through trees,
Painting secrets with a gentle breeze.

Golden rays pierce through the gloom,
Chasing darkness, dispelling doom,
Each flicker tells a deeper tale,
Where light and shadow softly sail.

Moments captured in quiet grace,
Echoes lingering in this space,
A canvas filled with soft delight,
The eternal play of day and night.

With every dawn, new hues arise,
Promises painted in the skies,
And as the sun begins to fall,
The shadows stretch, embracing all.

In this realm where contrasts meet,
Life's mysteries are bittersweet,
For every light that brightly glows,
There's a shadow that gently grows.

The Spark of Transcendent Beauty

A glimmer caught within the night,
A spark ignites, a fleeting light,
Moments woven, sheer and bright,
Transforming darkness into sight.

Love unfurls like petals wide,
In silence grows, cannot hide,
Breath of life in whispered form,
A beauty that can transform.

In laughter shared, the world ignites,
Each soul a flame, each heart a light,
Together we create the fire,
Burning fierce, endless desire.

With every touch, a magic rare,
A connection felt beyond compare,
In the heart where passion thrives,
The spark of beauty truly lives.

So let us chase this shining dream,
Embrace the light, let our hearts beam,
For in this dance of radiant glow,
We find the beauty that we know.

Brought to Light by the Fire

Embers flicker in the night air,
Whispers echo, secrets laid bare,
With every flame, a story told,
The warmth wrapping hearts like gold.

Crisp leaves rustle, shadows creep,
In the hearth, memories keep,
Each crackle sings a song of old,
Of courage found and fears controlled.

Gathered close, we feel the glow,
In the fire's dance, our spirits flow,
Voices rise like sparks above,
In this circle, we find our love.

As flames leap high, hearts are renewed,
A tapestry of dreams construed,
Brought to light by the fire's breath,
In the warmth, we conquer death.

So let the fire burn bright and bold,
For in its light, our stories unfold,
Together we cherish this sacred time,
Brought to life in rhythm and rhyme.

The Glorious Flame of Existence

In every heart, a flame ignites,
Burning fierce through darkest nights,
With passion's glow, we dance and sway,
The glorious flame lights up our way.

Boundless energy flows through dreams,
Life's essence woven into seams,
In laughter shared, we find our song,
To this fierce light, we all belong.

As time ticks forward, moments blaze,
A tapestry of earthly days,
In trials faced and in joy we find,
A brilliant fire, forever intertwined.

Each soul a spark in this grand scheme,
Together weaving hope and dream,
As we forge paths through time and space,
Unyielding flames, a bright embrace.

And when the shadows threaten to creep,
Our spirit's fire shall never sleep,
For in the dance of life we see,
The glorious flame, forever free.

Tapestry of Glistening Hopes

In the dawn's gentle light, we weave,
Threads of dreams that we believe.
Each stitch a whisper, soft and pure,
Binding hearts with hopes that endure.

Colors blend in a fragrant dance,
Every shimmer a fleeting chance.
Together we stand, united in glow,
A tapestry rich with love's overflow.

The weaver's hand, steady and wise,
Crafts a canvas where hope never dies.
With every knot, our spirits rise,
In this fabric, our future lies.

Golden threads, silver beams,
Framed in laughter, coated with dreams.
In every fold, stories unfold,
As we journey, our hearts bold.

Let us cherish this moment shared,
In shadows cast, we are prepared.
For in this tapestry of our making,
A legacy of hope, never breaking.

The Firebird's Lament

In the twilight's fading glow,
A firebird sings, its heart aglow.
With every note, a story weaves,
Of love once lost, and whispered leaves.

Through the night, its tears will fall,
Echoing softly, a haunting call.
Flames of passion, now turned to ash,
In silence lingers, a ghostly flash.

Time has flown on swiftest wings,
Yet in its heart, the sorrow clings.
The embers dance in the moonlight's embrace,
A fading spirit in life's race.

Once it soared, a blazing sight,
Now shadows flicker, lost from light.
In each lament, a dream deferred,
The silent night, the heart's unheard.

Still it sings, a fragile tune,
An aching voice beneath the moon.
For every flight that ends in pain,
A soul reborn, yet lost again.

Stirrings of Celestial Heat

Beneath the stars, where silence reigns,
Awakens warmth in cosmic veins.
A dance of light, both fierce and bright,
Stirrings of hearts ignite the night.

From distant worlds, the whispers flow,
Tides of passion, ebb and glow.
In every spark, a universe dreams,
Of endless love, in radiant beams.

Galaxies spin in graceful arcs,
While comets trace their fiery marks.
In this realm, where shadows meet,
We are drawn by celestial heat.

Embers of passion, fiercely alive,
In the dark, our spirits thrive.
Bound together, by fate's own thread,
In the warmth of words unsaid.

So let the night be our embrace,
A cosmic dance, in time and space.
With every heartbeat, we proclaim,
In the depths of stars, we are the same.

Fitness of Elysian Flames

In gardens lush, where dreams take flight,
Elysian flames burn warm and bright.
With every spark, desires bloom,
In the glow, dispel the gloom.

The winds whisper through gilded leaves,
As the heart seeks what it believes.
In sacred fire, our souls entwine,
Crafting beauty by design.

Every flicker tells a tale,
Of love refined, of hearts that sail.
Through trials faced and shadows cast,
These flames will forge a bond that lasts.

In the dance of passion, we ignite,
A symphony of heat and light.
In every ember, promise sways,
As the night transforms into days.

So let us stoke this sacred blaze,
In harmony, we find our ways.
With each heartbeat, with every sigh,
Together, we'll light the endless sky.

Inner Radiance and Its Shadows

In the depths of quiet night,
Flickers of light dance so bright.
Shadows whisper secrets low,
In the warmth of inner glow.

Veils of doubt sometimes draw near,
Yet the heart will still persevere.
In the storm, the calm abides,
Where the hidden truth resides.

Each choice reflects a beacon's beam,
Casting light on faded dreams.
Through the dark, the spirit strides,
Finding strength where love confides.

Inner radiance shines so clear,
Guiding paths we hold most dear.
Though shadows loom and winds may wail,
In our hearts, the light will prevail.

A journey carved from every scar,
Radiates like a distant star.
In the silence, echoes grow,
Inner light is all we know.

In the Heart of Every Ember

In the glow of dying fire,
Whispers tell of fierce desire.
Each ember tells a tale of old,
A story wrapped in warmth and gold.

Tangled threads of heat and ash,
Spark a flicker, hopes that flash.
In the heart of every spark,
Lies a flame that fights the dark.

Memories dance on fleeting light,
Holding moments, pure delight.
Every ember, soft and bright,
Reminds us of our inner fight.

With every breath, the warmth expands,
Embers pulse like heartbeats' bands.
In the silence, flames will rise,
Igniting dreams under vast skies.

Blaze of courage, burn so true,
In every heart, a flame will brew.
From the quiet, whispers fester,
Love ignites in every gesture.

Flames of the Unsung

In the depths of silent night,
Quiet passions take to flight.
Flames that flicker, whispers weak,
Speak of dreams that hearts can seek.

Unsung heroes, tales untold,
Burning bright, yet never bold.
In the shadows, voices stir,
Writing stories that concur.

Through the dark, they've made their way,
In every night, they find the day.
Undeterred by fleeting doubt,
They carry hope, their voices shout.

Fires of kindness, warmth they share,
In the stillness, they lay bare.
Fueling hope with gentle grace,
In every heart, they find their place.

Let their flames forever shine,
Echoing through the hands of time.
For in the unsung lies the truth,
A blazing light of endless youth.

The Pulse of Warm Wishes

In the stillness of the night,
Wishes travel, taking flight.
Carried on the winds of chance,
Spreading warmth in every glance.

A heartbeat wrapped in gentle care,
In every wish, a love laid bare.
Though unseen, they find a voice,
In the silence, hearts rejoice.

Threads of hope interlace tight,
Binding dreams with purest light.
With each breath, affection swells,
Painting stories only time tells.

Wishes beat like drums of old,
Tales of love, so brave and bold.
In the pulse of every heart,
We find the strength to never part.

So send your wishes on the breeze,
Let them dance among the leaves.
For in each pulse of warm desire,
Lives the spark of endless fire.

Flames of Forgotten Dreams

In shadows deep where visions fade,
Old wishes drift like soft parade.
The embers of hope softly sigh,
While stars above whisper goodbye.

Echoes linger in the night,
Fading whispers lost from sight.
Dreams once bold now lie in ash,
Time moves on, a fleeting flash.

Memories dance in twilight's grace,
A ghostly waltz, an empty space.
Yet in the heart, a spark remains,
A flicker bright that still sustains.

Through shadows cast and silent tears,
Life reclaims what once held fears.
As new dawns break with gentle light,
Flames revived, take off in flight.

In every loss, a lesson learned,
From ashes, brighter hopes can be turned.
So rise again, let dreams ignite,
With every flame, reclaim your night.

Resonance of the Inner Glow

Deep within where silence speaks,
A radiant voice the soul seeks.
Whispers gentle, soft like dawn,
Nurturing what makes us strong.

The universe within our reach,
With every lesson, life can teach.
In rhythms of the heart's embrace,
We find our true and sacred space.

As shadows dance with fleeting light,
Hope emerges, a beacon bright.
The inner glow, a steady flame,
Whispers softly, call your name.

Let each heartbeat sing the song,
Of love's embrace, where we belong.
In every note, a truth unfolds,
The resonance of dreams retold.

So feel the pulse, let spirit soar,
Through every challenge, seek the core.
For in the depths, we find our way,
And shine much brighter every day.

Flickers of the Heart's Passion

In gentle hush, the heartbeats call,
Flickers dance like fireflies small.
Whispers woven, soft and sweet,
The rhythm of love, our steady beat.

From tender glances, sparks arise,
Igniting dreams beneath the skies.
Each moment cherished, held so dear,
With every sigh, we draw you near.

Through storms that shake and winds that blow,
The flickers shine, they ebb and flow.
A tapestry of moments spun,
Together forever, two become one.

In twilight's embrace, our spirits meet,
With every heartbeat, a new heartbeat.
For in the flame, a love so bright,
Keeps us warm through darkest night.

The passion flows, a river grand,
United always, hand in hand.
Let flickers rise, let shadows fall,
In the glow of love, we have it all.

The Lament of Silent Sparks

In quiet nights, the sparks lament,
For dreams once bright, now slowly spent.
Whispers fade into the dark,
Yearning still, each hidden spark.

In shadows cast, the memories sigh,
Fragments of laughter, moments nigh.
Faded echoes, lost in time,
A melody with no more rhyme.

Yet in the silence, hope resides,
A flickering flame that quietly bides.
For every spark that fades away,
A new beginning finds its way.

Through depths of loss, we find the way,
Let silent sparks guide us to play.
For in the heart, resilience grows,
As tears transform and love bestows.

Let not despair hold back the light,
For every ending births a flight.
In every loss, a chance to see,
The silent sparks will set us free.

Tides of Illuminated Dreams

Beneath the starry sky so wide,
Waves of hope in silence glide.
Whispers of light, gentle and true,
Carrying wishes born anew.

In the heart, a beacon glows,
Illuminating paths we chose.
With every tide that ebbs and flows,
Our dreams take flight, as courage grows.

Along the shore where shadows play,
New horizons beckon, day by day.
The moon reflects our silent fears,
Yet also guides with light through tears.

Life's canvas painted in shades of night,
Colorful visions bathe in light.
Each wave a promise, each turn a chance,
In the dance of tides, our spirits prance.

As dawn breaks free, we rise once more,
With every wave, we learn to soar.
Carried by currents strong and bold,
Tides of dreams will never fold.

Whirling Fires of Memory

In the hearth where embers glow,
Flickers dance, soft and slow.
Stories born from past's embrace,
Carved in time, each line a trace.

Colors blend, a vivid flash,
Moments fade, yet hearts will clash.
Every spark a tale to tell,
In the whirling flames, we dwell.

Through golden hours, shadows weave,
Memories old, we still believe.
Flames may flicker, but never die,
In the warmth of love, we sigh.

Fires of youth, a fiery chase,
Guiding us through time and space.
With every breath, the past ignites,
In the night, our spirit lights.

As time unfolds, we stand apart,
Whirling dreams linger in the heart.
Through ashes grey and glowing bright,
Memory's dance is pure delight.

The Resilient Glow

Amidst the storms, we hold our ground,
Through valleys deep, our strength is found.
With every challenge, we shall rise,
In the face of doubt, we seek the skies.

A flicker bright, the ember's flame,
In every heart resides the same.
The strength we carry, bold and true,
In darkness, still, our light shines through.

Every setback fuels the fire,
Resilient souls never tire.
Bound by hope, our spirits soar,
In unity, we crave for more.

With passion fierce, our dreams ignite,
In the tapestry of day and night.
Each setback a step, each bruise a star,
In the journey ahead, we wander far.

The resilient glow, forever bright,
Guides us softly into the night.
Together we stand, hearts aglow,
In the dance of life, we bravely go.

Gusts of Shimmering Ambition

In the breeze that whispers low,
Ambitions rise, a gentle flow.
Carried forth on winds of change,
New horizons we will arrange.

With every gust, our spirits soar,
Dreams unbound, we aim for more.
Chasing visions, bold and bright,
In the flight of time, we find our light.

Storms may come, but still we stand,
Guided by hope, a steady hand.
Through the chaos, finding grace,
In the dance of goals, we find our place.

Shimmering dreams, like stars aglow,
Fueling passion, feeding the flow.
With every challenge, we become,
An unstoppable force, we hum.

In the currents, fierce and strong,
We find our mission, where we belong.
Gusts of ambition, wild and free,
In the tapestry of life, we see.

The Warmth of Hidden Yearnings

In the shadows where dreams lie,
Whispers echo, gently sigh.
Hearts aflame with secret fire,
Yearning souls that never tire.

Underneath the moonlit veil,
Hopeful hearts begin to sail.
Searching for a spark divine,
In the depths, our spirits shine.

In the silence, visions bloom,
Breath of life within the gloom.
Navigating through the night,
Guided by the inner light.

Craving warmth, a soft embrace,
Finding solace in this space.
Tender touches, silent pleas,
Fulfillment found upon the breeze.

As dawn breaks, the shadows fade,
Yearnings spoken, fears delayed.
With each moment that we share,
True connection fills the air.

Chasing the Whispering Light

Dancing through the gentle glade,
Golden rays in colors played.
Chasing whispers on the breeze,
Wandering where the heart finds ease.

Footsteps light on paths of chance,
Each soft breath, a serendipity dance.
With the dawn, hopes take their flight,
Chasing ever bright, the light.

Through the woods, delighted hearts,
Tracing where the magic starts.
Shadows curl, and sunlight weaves,
In this dance, our spirit believes.

Round the bend, the echoes call,
Blissful laughter fills the hall.
Running fast, we feel alive,
In this chase, our dreams revive.

Embrace the glow that fills the sky,
Hold on tight, do not be shy.
With each step, we find our way,
To the light that bids us stay.

Traces of the Heart's Brightness

In the quiet folds of night,
Hearts reveal their hidden light.
Soft reflections in the dark,
Shining brightly, leaving marks.

Moments linger, shadows dance,
Glimmers of a sweet romance.
Every glance a story told,
Traces of love, bright and bold.

Echoes linger in the air,
Whispers of our souls laid bare.
Lost in dreams, our spirits soar,
Mapping pathways to the core.

When the world feels cold and grey,
Brightness guides us on our way.
In the stillness, hearts unite,
Filling voids with pure delight.

Hand in hand, we journey on,
Fading doubts, a brand new dawn.
Sunrise glows, our souls ignite,
Radiant traces of our light.

Luminescence of the Unseen

In the depths where silence dwells,
Magic stirs and softly swells.
Hidden realms begin to gleam,
Fleeting light, a distant dream.

Caught between the stars and seas,
Something stirs upon the breeze.
A glow that dances, wise and free,
Illuminates our destiny.

In the shadows, secrets twine,
Whispers of the divine align.
Softly woven, threads of fate,
Luminous paths that draw us straight.

Through the veil, we seek to find,
Glimmers of the sacred mind.
In the depths where silence sings,
Shadows bloom like unseen wings.

As we walk through night's embrace,
Every step, a sacred trace.
Finding light where it has been,
Seeking joy in the unseen.

The Journey Through Fiery Hues

Through valleys deep and mountains high,
We wander forth beneath the sky.
With every step, colors unfold,
In fiery hues, stories told.

The sun dips low, an orange dream,
Whispers of hope in every beam.
A dance of light, a vibrant play,
Guiding us on our winding way.

Crimson leaves kiss the autumn air,
Each moment felt, beyond compare.
The road ahead, though dark and wide,
Ignites our souls, we walk with pride.

With every turn, a lesson learned,
Through gentle flames, our spirits burned.
The journey flows, heartbeats in sync,
Painting life's canvas with every blink.

Pathways of the Heart's Radiant Glow

Along the path where shadows dance,
We find the light in every chance.
With hearts aglow, we share our dream,
Paths intertwine like a flowing stream.

In silent whispers, love ignites,
Guiding us through the darkest nights.
Soft echoes of laughter fill the air,
Creating warmth wherever we care.

Every moment, a treasure cherished,
In the glow of love, fear is perished.
Together we walk through thick and thin,
With faith in our hearts, we rise, we win.

From dusk till dawn, our spirits soar,
Each heartbeat sings, forevermore.
Connected souls, a radiant show,
Keenly we travel, the heart's warm glow.

Flames Beneath the Surface

Underneath the calm facade,
Lies a fire, fierce and broad.
Smoldering thoughts, bright desires,
A world alive with hidden fires.

Each glance reveals a burning spark,
Resilient hearts that beat in dark.
Through quiet sighs and fleeting time,
We chase the shadows, truth in rhyme.

In stillness found, the warmth ignites,
Filling the voids with dazzling lights.
With every breath, a flame anew,
Strength from within, we break on through.

Beneath the waves of life's great sea,
Flames flicker, wild and free.
From ashes rise, we claim our worth,
In fire's embrace, we find rebirth.

The Ember's Testament

In every ember, a story glows,
Whispers of fire that nature knows.
A testament to battles fought,
In flickering lights, lessons taught.

The warmth of past, the heat of pain,
In quiet moments, we sustain.
With glowing hearts, we light our way,
Guided by embers that won't sway.

From ashes rise, with strength anew,
Embers dance, igniting the true.
Each flicker tells of love and loss,
In every spark, we bear our cross.

So hold the fire, let it beam,
In darkness found, together we dream.
The ember's glow, both fierce and warm,
A legacy born from every storm.

Shimmers of Wandering Desires

In twilight's gentle embrace,
Whispers of dreams take pace.
Stars flicker in the night,
Guiding hearts towards the light.

Journeys weave through sighs,
Painting hopes in the skies.
Chasing shadows of the past,
Yearning for a love to last.

Every heartbeat holds a clue,
Of the paths we wish to pursue.
Footsteps echo soft and clear,
In the realms where wishes steer.

Through valleys of untamed grace,
We seek a warm, familiar place.
With every shuddered breath we take,
Wandering desires never break.

And as the dawn unfurls its rays,
Illuminating hopeful ways,
The shimmers dance in the air,
Whispers of longing everywhere.

Reverberations of Blazing Truth

Beneath the roar of raging flames,
Truth's fierce glow ignites our names.
In shadows bright and shadows dark,
The heart ignites a sacred spark.

A tempest roars in the night,
Guiding souls toward the light.
Profound echoes filled with grace,
Resonating in this place.

With every clash, our spirits rise,
Burning doubts and bold alibis.
We stand firm, unyielding, free,
Together, we shape destiny.

In the silence of the storm,
We find the way to transform.
The blazing truth never hides,
In reverberations, hope abides.

As embers fall like whispered vows,
We burn and bend, we break our bows.
With every heartbeat, we reclaim,
The power of truth, our eternal flame.

Cradled by Warmth

In the embrace of a gentle night,
Dreams take flight in soft moonlight.
Wrapped in a melody so sweet,
With love's warmth, our hearts repeat.

Whispers dance upon the breeze,
Laughter blended with rustling leaves.
Safe in the arms that hold us tight,
We find solace in pure delight.

Each heartbeat echoes tender views,
A tapestry of timeless hues.
With eyes closed, we drift away,
Cradled by warmth, in sweet ballet.

Sunset paints the world in gold,
In these moments, hearts unfold.
Every sigh, a soothing balm,
Nestled close, our world is calm.

When shadows creep and twilight falls,
Love's embrace forever calls.
Together, we rise, we transform,
In the cradle of love's warm norm.

The Flame's Soft Soliloquy

In flickering glow, secrets sigh,
The flame holds tales that never die.
With every flicker, stories bloom,
In the quiet of the cozy room.

Soft whispers travel through the air,
Carrying warmth that bids us share.
Tales of lovers, lost and found,
In soft soliloquy, they resound.

Each spark ignites a precious thought,
Moments rendered, never caught.
In the breath of midnight's kiss,
We find solace, perfect bliss.

The fire crackles, a gentle tune,
Hearts entwined beneath the moon.
Embers dance, our dreams ignite,
The flame's soliloquy feels just right.

With patience, the night unfolds,
In stories whispered, love retolds.
Through every flame, our hopes fly high,
In the soft rhythms of a starlit sky.

The Last Whisper of a Candle

In darkness deep, a flicker glows,
A soft embrace where shadow flows.
The gentle wax drips slow and warm,
Its quiet dance, a love's sweet charm.

The night holds breath, as silence sighs,
While dreams are lit in fleeting ties.
A ghostly pulse, the flame's soft song,
A whisper frail, to night belongs.

Each shimmer fades with time's swift hand,
Echoes lost in night's vast land.
Yet in the heart, a memory stays,
Of candlelight in bygone days.

As embers dim and shadows creep,
The last farewell, the candle weeps.
A final glow, an end to light,
The whisper fades into the night.

Traces of Light in the Abyss

In the vast void where silence reigns,
Faint glimmers spark like whispered gains.
Among the dark, a hope ignites,
Painting dreams in fragile nights.

Stars twinkle soft, their ancient tales,
Fleeting moments, like fragile sails.
Each trace of light, a story spun,
A dance of shadows, the battle won.

Through unknown depths, the journey bends,
A search for warmth as silence ends.
Yet every spark, though far away,
Keeps despair's cold and dark at bay.

The abyss holds both fear and grace,
In stillness found, we find our place.
A flicker shines, a guide in gloom,
Traces of light, dispelling doom.

Threads of Heat and Light

Across the loom where moments weave,
Threads of warmth that we believe.
Every color sings a sound,
In the fabric of love, we are bound.

Heat of summers, bright and bold,
Stories shared and secrets told.
Every glance, a vibrant line,
Weaving destinies intertwined.

In the winter's chill, we find the spark,
Threads of light that pierce the dark.
Cocooned in hopes, together tight,
Love's embrace brings endless light.

As seasons change, our threads remain,
Heat of memories, joy, and pain.
Together spun, this tapestry,
Threads of heat and light set free.

The Glimmer of Forgotten Flames

In dusty rooms where echoes dwell,
Whispers linger, tales to tell.
Once bright spirits, now but dreams,
The glimmer fades, or so it seems.

Yet in the shadows, hints arise,
Faint flickers dance beneath the skies.
The heartbeat of a brighter time,
A memory wrapped in softly rhyme.

As embers cool, they do not die,
But rest and wait for wings to fly.
A quiet spark, a secret kept,
In the soul's heart, where love has slept.

So when the night feels cold and long,
Remember sweet the ancients' song.
For in the dark, where hope refrains,
There lies the glimmer of forgotten flames.

Whispers of a Fiery Heart

In the quiet, embers glow,
Softly speaking truths we know.
Passion flickers in the night,
A tender blaze, a warming light.

Through the silence, sparks arise,
Breathing warmth beneath the skies.
Yearning souls, a dance of fire,
Weaving dreams, igniting desire.

Hearts entwined in whispered flame,
Secrets spoken, never the same.
Burning brightly, never shy,
In these moments, we learn to fly.

Crimson threads through endless dark,
Each heartbeat, a glowing mark.
With every breath, the passion stays,
Guiding us through life's fierce maze.

From ashes rise, our spirits free,
Dancing shadows, wild and glee.
Whispers echo in the night,
A fiery heart, forever bright.

Shadows of Inner Light

In the depths, where shadows play,
Flickering thoughts begin to sway.
Quiet whispers, softly call,
Guiding shadows, through it all.

Glimmers dance on edges dim,
Filling voids, where hopes begin.
Each heartbeat casts a gentle beam,
Illuminating every dream.

Light within, an ancient spark,
Burning bright within the dark.
Fleeting moments, tender grace,
A refuge found in this place.

Veils of doubt may linger long,
Yet inner light, forever strong.
Through the shadows, love does lead,
Nurturing the darkest seed.

From the hidden, truths arise,
Lighting paths beneath the skies.
Shadows dance, the heart does sing,
Embracing all that light can bring.

Reflections in the Ember

In the hearth, the embers glow,
Casting warmth in evening's flow.
Each reflection shows a part,
Whispers echo in the heart.

Memories flicker, soft and bright,
Reminders of the love and light.
In every spark, a story clear,
Echoes of those held so dear.

Fleeting flames, they come, they go,
Yet in stillness, feelings grow.
From the ashes, hope reborn,
In the light of every morn.

Embers dance, a silent cheer,
Holding whispers close and near.
In those moments, truth is found,
A sacred space, love unbound.

Through the fire, our spirits soar,
Every heartbeat, wanting more.
Reflections warm our darkest night,
In the ember, lies our light.

Luminous Murmurs

In twilight's grasp, our voices blend,
Luminous murmurs, whispers tend.
Each soft note a thread of gold,
Tales of love and dreams retold.

Dancing light in gentle sway,
Guided by the night's ballet.
In serene glow, hearts entwine,
A harmony both sweet and fine.

Every breath, a song of peace,
In this moment, worries cease.
With every flicker, courage found,
In luminous whispers, we are bound.

Starlit skies, our canvas bright,
Painting dreams in shades of light.
Through the darkness, love's embrace,
Finding hope in tender grace.

Murmurs echo through the night,
Casting shadows, warming bright.
In this dance of souls, we see,
Luminous whispers set us free.

Whispers of the Heart's Inferno

In the depths where secrets lie,
Softly murmurs, a painful sigh.
Fires flicker, stories unfold,
Whispers weave, in shadows bold.

Embers dance beneath the skin,
Churning thoughts, where dreams begin.
A heartbeat echoes, wild and free,
In the flames, my soul shall be.

Remembered tales, both dark and bright,
Fuel the passion, ignite the night.
Burning brightly, love's fierce call,
In this inferno, I risk it all.

Through the chaos, I find my way,
In the ashes, hope won't sway.
Every whisper, a sacred part,
Beckons me, the heart's true art.

With every blaze, I lose and gain,
From the fire, I rise from pain.
In the embers' glow, I find my worth,
Whispers linger, rebirth on earth.

Shadows of the Inner Fire

In the quiet of the night,
Shadows dance, a flickering light.
Fire within, a gentle spark,
Guides me through the deepening dark.

Veiled in mist, my thoughts take flight,
Chasing dreams till morning light.
Beneath the surface, embers gleam,
Burning softly, fueled by dream.

Each shadow tells a tale to share,
Of battles fought and hearts laid bare.
Through the flame, my spirit soars,
Unlocking all the hidden doors.

Moments lost, and moments found,
In the silence, strength unbound.
Courage builds in whispered tones,
Inner fire, I claim my bones.

As dawn approaches, shadows fade,
Yet the fire, I cannot trade.
In its glow, I stand as one,
Beneath the stars, my journey's done.

Reflections of the Spirit's Light

In the mirror of the soul's embrace,
Shimmers light, a sacred space.
Illuminating paths and scars,
Guiding journeys among the stars.

Each flicker, a whisper of the past,
Reflections dance, shadows cast.
Through the trials, a spirit shines,
In the darkness, love defines.

In every heartbeat, light is found,
Beneath the surface, hope unbound.
Resilience blooms, like flowers bright,
In the garden of the spirit's light.

Moments cherished, fragile and bold,
Stories layered, memories gold.
Through the lens of what has been,
A brighter future waits within.

As seasons change, the light remains,
Guiding through joy and through pains.
In every reflection, a journey anew,
Spirit's light, forever true.

The Dance of Eternal Embers

In the night, where dreamers play,
Eternal embers light the way.
Dancing flames, both wild and free,
Whispering tales of destiny.

Each flicker holds a memory dear,
Old and new, both far and near.
As they swirl in the moonlit air,
I find solace, beyond despair.

With every dance, a heartbeat shares,
Stories woven with tender cares.
In the rhythm, passion speaks,
Binding spirits, the lost and meek.

Through the fire, shadows twine,
Forever joined, your hand in mine.
In the dance of eternal light,
We ignite, dispelling the night.

So let us sway through the cosmic glow,
In this dance, our spirits flow.
For in the embers, love ignites,
A timeless dance of heart's delights.

Kindling the Spirit's Desire

In the quiet dawn, dreams arise,
Whispers of hope, beneath the skies.
A flicker of light, a spark so bright,
Awakening hearts, igniting the night.

With every breath, the longing grows,
Fueling the fire, as passion shows.
A dance of souls, beneath the stars,
Embracing the warmth, erasing the scars.

Embers of courage, softly they glow,
Guiding our path, as forward we go.
Through trials faced, our spirits entwine,
Kindling the flame, a love divine.

In laughter shared, in tears we weave,
Stories of strength, in moments we grieve.
Each heartbeat echoes, a rhythmic sigh,
A journey of trust, together we fly.

So let us nurture, this fire inside,
For in the dark, it will be our guide.
Through every storm, we'll stand so tall,
Kindling the spirit, answering the call.

A Tapestry of Light and Heat

Woven in colors, bright and bold,
Stories of warmth, in threads of gold.
Each hue a memory, each stitch a dream,
In a tapestry of love, forever gleam.

The shimmer of laughter, the glow of a smile,
Embraced in comfort, we stay awhile.
Together we gather, in the warmth we find,
A fabric of hearts, beautifully entwined.

In moments cherished, our souls will soar,
Crafting a journey, an open door.
The light that flickers, the heat that stays,
Guiding our nights, through life's winding maze.

Threads of connection, strong and true,
Binding us closer, in all that we do.
Each pattern a promise, each knot a vow,
In the tapestry of life, here and now.

Through laughter's echo and silence profound,
We find our place, where love is found.
A radiant blend, our spirits unite,
In this tapestry of light and heat, we ignite.

Threads of the Heart's Fire

In the fabric of time, our stories thread,
Woven with passion, the tears we shed.
Each strand a whisper, a promise made,
In the warmth of the heart, never to fade.

Through trials faced, united we stand,
Holding onto dreams, a gentle hand.
The fire within, a blazing spark,
Illuminating paths, lighting the dark.

In every heartbeat, the rhythm flows,
Binding our spirits, as love grows.
With threads of courage, stitched with grace,
We create a tapestry, a sacred space.

Each flicker a memory, cherished and bright,
In the dance of the flames, we find our light.
Together we weave, our lives entwined,
Threads of the heart's fire, beautifully aligned.

For even in shadows, our love will remain,
A testament everlasting, through joy and pain.
So let the flames rise, let them inspire,
As we journey together, threads of fire.

Beneath the Surface of the Flame

In the flicker of night, secrets unfold,
Whispers of warmth in embers of gold.
Beneath the surface, the heat resides,
Stirring the depths where passion abides.

With every glow, the truth ignites,
A dance of shadows, in flickering lights.
The warmth of connection, softly revealed,
In the heart's quiet fire, our fate is sealed.

In moments paused, in silence we find,
Resonance deep, the ties that bind.
Beneath the flame, our spirits entwine,
An everlasting glow, beautifully divine.

Through tales of desire, etched in the night,
We venture forward, toward the light.
In the depths of our souls, the fire won't wane,
Beneath the surface, we dance in the flame.

So let the embers carry our dreams,
In the warmth of love, everything gleams.
Beneath the surface, where hope ignites,
We journey together, into the nights.

Dances on the Surface of Fire

Flames flicker in the night,
Casting shadows, dark and bright.
Whispers of heat, a gentle sigh,
A fiery dance, beneath the sky.

Spirits twirl in orange glow,
Embers leap, a vibrant show.
Moments slip like grains of sand,
In this realm, we take a stand.

Hearts ignite in passion's chase,
Finding life in burning space.
Fury swirls as breathless night,
Laces dance with flickers of light.

Crimson trails and molten streams,
Echo softly hidden dreams.
As flames embrace the fleeting air,
We lose ourselves in what we share.

Time dissolves in heat's embrace,
In this wild, untamed place.
The fire speaks a language vast,
In every crackle, beats the past.

Silence of the Glowing Truth

In quiet glow, the truth resides,
Whispers soft, like gentle tides.
Hidden depths, a silent song,
In the stillness, we belong.

Shadows dance on walls pristine,
Underneath the silver sheen.
Each moment speaks without a sound,
In the calm, our hopes are found.

Eyes reflect a restful light,
Carrying dreams through the night.
In this hush, we touch the skies,
Listening close to what life implies.

Every heartbeat syncs in time,
Nature's pulse, a soft rhyme.
Secrets wrapped in tender grace,
In silence, we find our place.

Timeless echoes softly blend,
In the stillness, hearts transcend.
The glowing truth, a gentle guide,
In quiet spaces, love abides.

Beneath the Ashen Veil

Underneath the smokey haze,
Lost in thoughts of distant days.
A veil of ash, a blanket cold,
Whispers of stories left untold.

Embers flicker, shadows creep,
Secrets buried, dreams asleep.
Life pulsates beneath the grit,
In the lost, new seeds are lit.

Time holds on with weary grace,
Each memory, a fragile trace.
Beneath the weight, we yearn to rise,
To uncover truth in dusky skies.

Yet hope glimmers through the gray,
A spark that won't fade away.
With every breath, we find a way,
To lift the ash, and greet the day.

Emerging from the shadows dense,
We reclaim joy, make amends.
Within the veil, a chance to see,
Life anew, a sacred decree.

The Dance of Luminous Shadows

In twilight's grasp, shadows play,
Flickering forms that sway and stay.
Chasing light through the darkened lane,
A dance unfolds, both joy and pain.

Figures twirl in whispered grace,
Every movement finds its place.
Illuminated by the moon's kiss,
A fleeting moment, a tender bliss.

Colors shift and softly blend,
In this realm, we start to mend.
Luminous shadows intertwine,
Crafting stories, line by line.

With every step, the echoes call,
Learning to rise, learning to fall.
In the shadows, we find our light,
An endless dance, both bold and bright.

Together we weave, together we soar,
Endless rhythms, forever more.
In this ballet of dark and shine,
The dance of shadows, yours and mine.

9 781805 617556